First World War
and Army of Occupation
War Diary
France, Belgium and Germany

57 DIVISION
172 Infantry Brigade
Prince of Wales's Volunteers (South Lancashire Regiment)
2/5th Battalion
13 September 1915 - 24 February 1916

WO95/2985/9

The Naval & Military Press Ltd
www.nmarchive.com
Published in association with The National Archives

Published by

The Naval & Military Press Ltd

Unit 10 Ridgewood Industrial Park,
Uckfield, East Sussex,
TN22 5QE England
Tel: +44 (0) 1825 749494

www.naval-military-press.com

www.nmarchive.com

This diary has been reprinted in facsimile from the original. Any imperfections are inevitably reproduced and the quality may fall short of modern type and cartographic standards.

© Crown Copyright
Images reproduced by permission of The National Archives, London, England, 2015.

Contents

Document type	Place/Title	Date From	Date To
Heading	WO95/2985/9 57 Divn: 172 Inf. Brig 2/5 5th Lancs Regt 1915 Sept-1916 Feb		
Miscellaneous	War Diary	31/08/1918	31/08/1918
Miscellaneous	War Diary	00/08/1915	00/08/1915
Heading	War Diary Headquarters 2/5th Battalion South Lancashire Regiment Tandridge Camp Oxted Period September 1st To September 30th 1915		
War Diary	Tandridge Camp Oxted	13/09/1915	30/09/1915
Heading	War Diary 2/5th Battalion South Lancashire Regiment Period October 1st 1915 To October 31st 1915		
War Diary	Oxted	04/10/1915	31/10/1915
Heading	War Diary And Summary Of Events And Information 2/5th Battalion South Lancashire Regiment Period November 1st 1915 To November 30th 1915		
War Diary	Maidstone	01/11/1915	30/11/1915
Heading	War Diary 2/5th Bn South Lancs Regt Period December 1st 1915 To December 31st 1915		
War Diary	Maidstone	01/12/1915	31/12/1915
Heading	War Diary 2/5th Bn South Lancashire Regiment Period From January 1st 1916 To January 31st 1916.		
War Diary	Maidstone	03/01/1916	31/01/1916
Heading	War Diary 2/5th Battalion South Lancashire Regiment Period February 1st 1916 February 29th 1916		
War Diary	Maidstone	07/02/1916	24/02/1916

WO 95 2485/9

57 Divn: 172 Inf. Brig.
2/5 Sth Lancs Regt
1915 Sept - 1916 Feb.

WAR DIARY.

From 1st to 31st August, 1915.

Unit: 2/4th Battalion, South Lancashire Regiment.

Brigade: 172nd Infantry Brigade.

Division: 57th (West Lancs) Division.

Mobilisation Centre:- WARRINGTON, LANCASHIRE.

Temporary Hqr Station:- OXTED, SURREY.

Stations since occupied subsequent to Concentration:
BLACKPOOL. TUNBRIDGE WELLS. ASHFORD.

MOVE. The Battalion, on change of Station, marched in four days (August 22nd to 25th) from ASHFORD to OXTED; distance about 46 miles.

1st Day's March:- from ASHFORD to HARRIETSHAM.
2nd Day's March:- from HARRIETSHAM to EAST MALLING.
3rd Day's March:- from EAST MALLING to SEAL.
4th Day's March:- from SEAL to OXTED.

The men bivouacked each night. Each day the cooks after dinner proceeded to the next halting place, drew rations from A.S.C, and prepared the dinner ready for the men when they marched in. Comparatively few men fell out during the march.

TRAINING. The training of the trained men is progressing and bayonet fighting has been largely practised. In consequence of the unit having received two drafts from the 3rd Line Unit, there are several groups of men in varying stages of efficiency.

DISCIPLINE. The discipline has improved since the Battalion has been under canvas.

ACCOMMODATION. A very large proportion of the tents taken over are in a very bad state of repair.

TRANSPORT. On the march from ASHFORD this section did very well; the whole journey being performed without a breakdown.

MESSING. This is being attended to very closely and is generally giving satisfaction.

DRAFTS. A draft of 140 men proceeded to join the 2/4th Battn South Lancashire Regiment in France at the beginning of the month, and three Officers at the end.

[signature] Lieut Colonel,
Commanding.
2/4th Bn South Lancashire Regiment.

WAR DIARY

August 1915

2/5th Battalion South Lancashire Regiment

MONTHLY SUMMARY OF WORK DONE & INSTRUCTION

UNIT 2/5th Battalion South Lancashire Regiment.

BRIGADE West Lancs. Brigade

DIVISION West (2nd. Lancs) Division.

ORGANIZATION Part of 2nd Army Central Force.

ADMINISTRATIVE CENTRE St Helens, Lancashire.

(a) LOCATION .... St. Helens 15.8.14.

(b) WORK ...

(c) MOVES ...

(d) OFFICERS ... joined

(e) OTHER RANKS ...

(f) TRAINING ... Grenadier Training has been the feature of the month.

J. Bates
LIEUT. COL
2/5TH BATTALION SOUTH LANC. REGT.

WAR DIARY

HEADQUARTERS

2/5th Battalion South Lancashire Regiment

TANDRIDGE CAMP.   OXTED

period

September 1st to September 30th 1915

and

SUMMARY OF EVENTS AND INFORMATION

Tandridge Camp.
  Oxted.
3rd October 1915.

Army Form C. 2118.

WAR DIARY
or
INTELLIGENCE SUMMARY.

(Erase heading not required.)

Instructions regarding War Diaries and Intelligence Summaries are contained in F.S. Regs., Part II. and the Staff Manual respectively. Title pages will be prepared in manuscript.

Hour, Date, Place	Summary of Events and Information	Remarks and references to Appendices
Tandridge Camp. Oxted. September 13th to 18th	Battalion engaged in digging on South London Defences.	
September 13th 1915	3 Officers proceeded to the Elementary Course of Instruction. Cambridge University.	
September 13th 1915	1 N.C.O. to Musketry Course of Instruction. Bisley.	
September 13th 1915	2 officers and 4 N.C.O's attended a local Musketry Course under Brigade Arrangements.	
September 13th 1915	Inspection of the Camp by the G.O.C. 2nd Army.	
September 16th 1915	4 New Army Officers joined this Unit under War Office order for attachment.	
September 21st 1915	1 N.C.O attended Infantry Pioneer Course Wrotham.	
September 24th 1915	3 Officers proceeded to Southampton en route for overseas as a reinforcing draft.	
September 27th to October 2nd 1915	Battalion engaged in digging on South London Defences	
September 30th 1915	STRENGTH Officers...................37 Other Ranks...............744	

TANDRIDGE CAMP.
OXTED. SURREY.
5TH OCTOBER 1915

.................O'Bain................Lieutenant-Colonel.
COMMANDING 2/5th Battalion South Lancashire Regiment.

WAR DIARY   OCTOBER 1915

HEADQUARTERS

2/5th Battalion South Lancashire Regiment

PERIOD

October 1st 1915

to

October 31st 1915

AND SUMMARY OF EVENTS AND INFORMATION

MEDWAY MILLS.
   MAIDSTONE
      4th November 1915.

Army Form C. 2118.

WAR DIARY
of
INTELLIGENCE SUMMARY
(Erase heading not required.)

OCTOBER 1915

Instructions regarding War Diaries and Intelligence Summaries are contained in F.S. Regs., Part II. and the Staff Manual respectively. Title pages will be prepared in manuscript.

Hour, Date, Place	Summary of Events and Information	Remarks and references to Appendices
Oxted. October 4th 1915.	One Officer to School of Instruction Sevenoaks.	
" 12th "	One Officer and one N.C.O. to Grenadier Course Godstone.	
" 14th "	One officer to School of Military Engineering Wrotham.	
" 18th "	One Officer to O.T.C. Junior Course of Instruction. Cambridge.	
" 18th "	One N.C.O. to 1st Grenadier Class at Wrotham.	
" 25th "	One N.C.O. to Musketry Course of Instruction Bisley.	
" 25th "	Four Officers to Junior O.T.C. Course Hereford.	
" 25th "	The Battalion changed Station from Oxted to Maidstone proceeding by March Route and arriving at Maidstone on October 26th.	
" 31st "	STRENGTH Officers................39. Other Ranks.............739.	
MAIDSTONE		

4th November 1915 COMMANDING 2/5th Battalion South Lancashire Regiment.

..........................Lieutenant-Colonel.

WAR DIARY

and

SUMMARY OF EVENTS AND INFORMATION

Headquarters
2/5th Battalion South Lancashire Regiment

PERIOD

November 1st 1915

to

November 30th 1915

Medway Mills
Maidstone
4th December 1915.

Army Form C. 2118.

WAR DIARY
INTELLIGENCE SUMMARY.

(Erase heading not required.)

November 1915.

Instructions regarding War Diaries and Intelligence Summaries are contained in F. S. Regs., Part II and the Staff Manual respectively. Title pages will be prepared in manuscript.

Hour, Date, Place		Summary of Events and Information	Remarks and references to Appendices
Maidstone	November 1st 1915	4 Field Kitchens received, also 2 limbered G.S. Wagons.	
	November 3rd 1915	1. N.C.O. proceeded to Veterinary Course of Instruction at Aylesford.	
	November 3rd 1915	1 officer proceeded to Grenadier Course of Instruction Hedstone.	
	November 9th 1915	1.N.C.O. proceeded to Pioneer Course of Instruction Wrotham.	
	November 9th 1915	2 Carts Water tank Mark V. received.	
	November 10th 1915	6. N.C.O's attended a Local Course of Instruction in Physical Training.	
	November 15th 1915	1. officer and 1NN.C.O proceeded to School of Trench Fighting at Wrotham.	
	November 15th 1915	1.N.C.O. proceeded to School of Cookery at Dartford.	
	November 16th 1915	2 officers and 4.N.C.O's attended a Local Course of Musketry Instruction.	
	November 17th 1915	2 officers proceeded to Junior Course of Instruction at Oxford University.	
	November 21st 1915	256 Rifles (525) withdrawn and returned to Weedon.	
	November 21st 1915	303 Rifles (525) Received from Weedon and issued.	
	November 23rd 1915	1.N.C.O. proceeded to School of Instruction in Cold Sgoeing at Bermondsey.	
	November 25th 1915	1 officer proceeded to Course of Instruction at Staff College Cember-ley.	
	November 26th 1915	The Band was disbanded and First Line men sent to 3rd Line.	
	November 27th 1915	Inspection of the Battalion by the Inspector of Infantry Central Force.	
	November 29th 1915	No report received.	
	November 29th 1915	1 officer and 1.N.C.O. proceeded to School of Trench Fighting at Wrotham.	
	November 29th 1915	1. N.C.O. proceeded to School of Cookery at Blackheath.	
	November 30th 1915	7 officers transferred to 3rd Line Depot.	
		(Authority. War Office Letter 9/Infantry/2 (T.F.3) dated 8th November 1915).	
	November 30th 1915	STRENGTH	
		Officers...............32.	
		Other Ranks...........708.	

MAIDSTONE ....Lieutenant-Colonel.
4th December 1915 COMMANDING 2/5th Battalion South Lancashire Regiment.

War Diary.

2/5th Bn South Lancs Regt

Period

December 1st 1915

to

December 31st 1915.

and Summary of Events
and Information

Medway. Mills.
Maidstone
5th January. 1916.

Army Form C. 2118.

WAR DIARY
or
INTELLIGENCE SUMMARY.
(Erase heading not required.)

DECEMBER 1915.

Hour, Date, Place 1915	Summary of Events and Information	Remarks and references to Appendices
Maidstone. December 1st	3 Officers transferred to 3rd Line Unit (Reduction of Strength as per War Office Letter 9/Infantry/2 (T.F.3) dated 8th November 1915)	
December 2nd	Visit by Major White Inspector of Messing.	
December 2nd	1 Officer to Infantry Pioneer Course Wrotham.	
December 6th	B.G.S. Limbered wagons received. All transport now Government pattern with the exception of the Officer's Mess Cart.	
December 11th	1 Range Finder Bar and Stroud and 1 Mekometer received.	
December 13th	4 N.C.O's to Local Physical Training Class.	
December 13th	1 N.C.O. to 2nd Army School of Trench Warfare. Wrotham.	
December 15th	Inspection of the Battalion by the G.O.C. 2nd Army. Company Drill Bayonet Fighting etc.	
December 16th	1 Officer transferred to Command Depot Heaton Park. Manchester.	
December 18th	2 Company Cooks sent to School of Cookery Dartford.	
December 21st	Inspection of the Battalion in Bayonet Fighting by the Assistant Inspector of Gymnasia.	
December 27th	1 Officer to 2nd Army School of Trench Warfare Wrotham.	
December 28th	2 Officers men to School of Cookery Bermondsey	
December 30th	Inspection of the Battalion in Musketry by Commandant School of Musketry	
December 30th	STRENGTH Officers..........29 Other Ranks.........682	

Maidstone
5.1.16

............................Captain for Lieut-Col
Commanding 1st Bn South Lancs Regiment

WAR DIARY.

HEADQUARTERS.

2/5th Bn South Lancashire Regiment.

P E R I O D

from

JANUARY 1st 1916.

to

JANUARY 31st 1916.

and

Summary of events and information.

Medway Mills.
Maidstone.
4-1-16.

WAR DIARY
or
INTELLIGENCE SUMMARY

(Erase heading not required.)

Army Form C. 2118

JANUARY 1916.

Instructions regarding War Diaries and Intelligence Summaries are contained in F.S. Regs., Part II. and the Staff Manual respectively. Title Pages will be prepared in manuscript.

Place	Date	Hour	Summary of Events and Information	Remarks and references to Appendices
Maid-stone.	Jany 3rd		3 N.C.O's to 2nd Army School for N.C.O's, Tunbridge Wells.	
			1 N.C.O. to Saddlers Course. TONBRIDGE.	
			1 N.C.O. to Musketry Course. Bisley.	
			Lt. Col. D. Bates attached for three days to B.E.F. in Flanders for instruction.	
	4th to 5th			
	5th		1 Officer and 1 NCO to Pioneer Course. Wrotham.	
	8th		1 NCO to Course of instruction in Minor Repairs and small arms. Enfield Lock.	
	10th		2 Officers and 1 NCO to 2nd Army School of Trench Warfare, Wrotham.	
			1 man to Course of Instruction in repair of Service bicycles. Woolwich.	
	22nd		First Batch of Derby Recruits posted ; 46 in number ; from O/C Admin. Centre. St Helens.	
	23rd		Second Batch of Derby Recruits posted; 37 in number; from O/C Admin. Centre. St Helens.	
	24th		3 NCO's to 2nd Army School for N.C.O's Tunbridge Wells.	
			1 Officer to Machine Gun Course at Bisley.	
			1 Officer to Musketry Course at Bisley.	
			1 NCO to 2nd Army School of Trench Warfare. Wrotham.	
			1 Officer to Company Officers Field Training class at Canterbury.	
	25th		Third Batch of Derby Recruits posted ; 46 in number; from O/C Admin. Centre. St Helens.	
			Fourth Batch of Derby Recruits posted ; 30 in number; from O/C Admin. Centre. St Helens.	
	25th		1 Officers & 2 N.C.O's to Pioneer Course. WROTHAM.	
	26th			
	31st		1 Officer to Company Officers Field training class at Canterbury.	
			STRENGTH.	
			Officers............28	
			Other Ranks..........829	
			[signature] Captain for Lt.Col.	
			Commanding 2/5th Bn South Lancashire Regiment.	
			(absent on leave).	
Maidstone.	2nd Feby 1916.			

WAR DIARY

HEADQUARTERS

2/5th Battalion South Lancashire Regiment.

PERIOD

from

February 1st 1916.

to

February 29th 1916.

and Summary of Events and Information.

Medway Mills.
 Maidstone.
  3rd March 1916.

Army Form C. 2118

WAR DIARY
or
INTELLIGENCE SUMMARY
(Erase heading not required.)

Instructions regarding War Diaries and Intelligence Summaries are contained in F. S. Regs., Part II. and the Staff Manual respectively. Title Pages will be prepared in manuscript.

Place	Date	Hour	Summary of Events and Information	Remarks and references to Appendices
Maidstone.	Feby 7th		1 Sergeant and 4 Lance Corporals and privates despatched to HOLLINGBOURN to take up duty as an Aerial Observation Post there.	A/1
	Feby 24th		The Battalion received orders to hold itself in readiness to move in case of an alarm.	A/1

MAIDSTONE.

2nd March 1916.

O Bates

............Lt. Colonel.

Commanding 2/5th Bn South Lancashire Regiment.